# Satellites

by Darlene R. Stille

Content Adviser: Professor Sherry L. Field, Department of Social Science Education, College of Education, The University of Georgia

Reading Adviser: Dr. Linda D. Labbo, Department of Reading Education, College of Education, The University of Georgia

**Compass Point Books**

Minneapolis, Minnesota

Compass Point Books
3722 West 50th Street, #115
Minneapolis, MN 55410

Visit Compass Point Books on the Internet at *www.compasspointbooks.com* or e-mail your request to *custserv@compasspointbooks.com*

Editors: E. Russell Primm and Emily J. Dolbear
Photo Researcher: Svetlana Zhurkina
Photo Selector: Catherine Neitge
Designer: Melissa Voda

**Library of Congress Cataloging-in-Publication Data**
Stille, Darlene R.
    Satellites / by Darlene R. Stille.
        p. cm. — (Let's see)
    Includes bibliographical references and index.
    ISBN 0-7565-0137-7
    1. Artificial satellites—Juvenile literature. [1. Artificial satellites.] I. Title.
TL796.3 .S85 2001
629.46—dc21                                    2001001449

# Table of Contents

# Blast Off!

Rumble, rumble. The ground is shaking. Boom! With a flash of fire and a loud roar, the huge rocket lifts slowly off its launchpad. It goes faster and faster, higher and higher.

This rocket is heading for space. It is carrying a satellite. The rocket lets go of the satellite. Then the satellite **orbits** Earth.

This satellite orbits very high above Earth. It goes around Earth so slowly that it looks like it is not moving at all.

Some satellites orbit close to Earth. These satellites go around Earth very fast. Some of them orbit Earth in less than two hours!

◄ *A rocket blasts into space carrying a communications satellite.*

# You Use Satellites Every Day

More than 2,000 satellites are now orbiting Earth. They do many jobs that help you. They help you see TV programs and make phone calls. If you get lost, satellites can even help you find your way.

Control centers on Earth can "talk" to a satellite. Computers in control centers send up radio signals. Then, computers on the satellite send radio signals back down to Earth. Satellite dish antennas act like big ears. They collect the signals from the satellite. A satellite gets power from the Sun. **Solar panels** catch sunlight and turn it into electricity.

◄ *The solar panels on the satellite give it power from the Sun.*

# The First of Many Satellites

The first satellite was called *Sputnik 1*. The Soviet Union sent it into orbit in 1957. The Soviet Union's second satellite was *Sputnik 2*. It carried a passenger. It was a dog named Laika.

The United States launched its first satellite in 1958. It was called *Explorer 1*. After that, many more satellites went into orbit. Companies as well as countries own satellites today.

◄ *The space shuttle's remote arm holds a satellite. The satellite is studying the Sun.*

# TV and Phone Calls from Space

Some telephone calls and television pictures "bounce" off communications satellites. These satellites have big antennas.

The telephone and TV signals go up to the satellite from one place on Earth. The satellite sends the signals down to another place on Earth. Think about satellites when you talk on the phone. Maybe your voice is "bouncing" off a satellite.

Do you have a satellite TV receiver? The signal comes right from the satellite to the dish on your roof. It then travels along a wire into the house and to your TV.

◀ *Huge satellite receivers sit on top of high-rise buildings.*

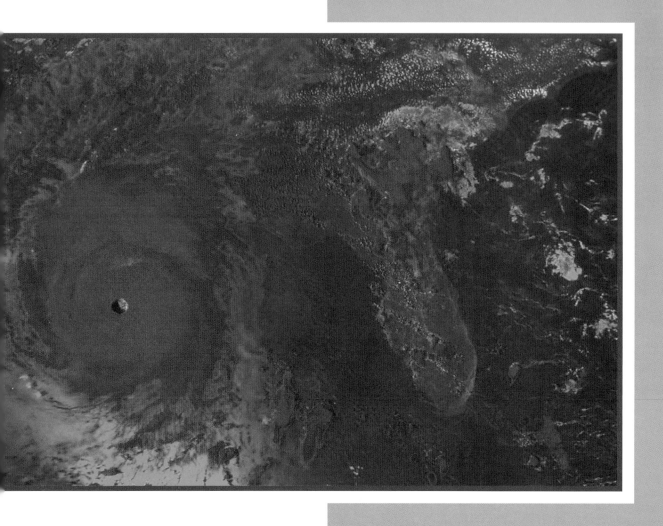

# Weather Satellites

Do you ever watch the weather reports on television? If so, you have seen pictures of clouds on Earth. These pictures come from weather satellites. Most weather satellites are in low orbit. They help us to predict storms and other kinds of weather on Earth.

◄ *A weather image from a satellite shows a hurricane in the Gulf of Mexico.*

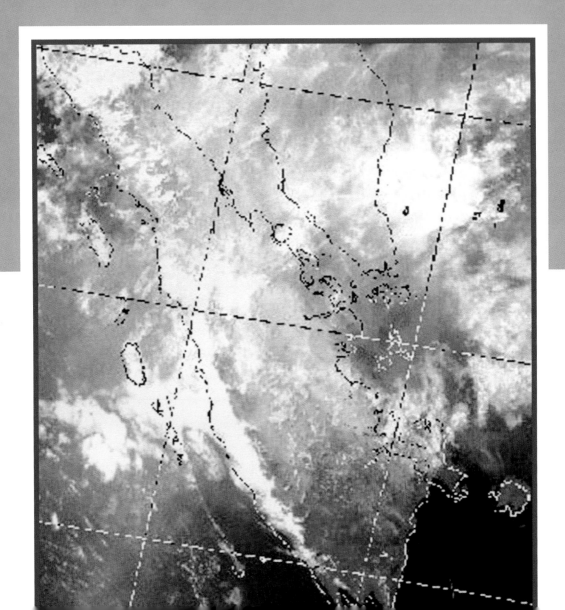

# Satellites That Study Earth

Some satellites look for pollution on Earth. This kind of satellite is called an Earth observation satellite. These satellites can see how much forestland is being used. They can tell scientists about farm crops.

Earth observation satellites can also find out how warm or cold the ocean is. They can tell us many things about our world.

◄ *Smoke from forest and brush fires in Indonesia can be seen clearly from outer space.*

# Satellites That Know Where You Are

Navigation satellites help planes in the air and ships at sea. These satellites keep planes and ships from getting lost.

Some navigation satellites can even help you if you are lost. You would have to take a special little computer with you though. The satellites send signals to this computer. Then the computer figures out where you are. This is called the **global positioning system** (GPS).

Some countries have spy satellites. Special cameras on spy satellites take close-up pictures of places on Earth.

◄ *This surveyer is wearing a GPS to find utilities buried underground.*

# Telescopes on Satellites

Some satellites carry telescopes. These telescopes look deep into space. They send back pictures of stars and **galaxies**. These telescopes in space help scientists study the universe.

Earth is a planet that orbits the Sun. Other planets orbit the sun too. We want to know more about these planets.

Sometimes we send a satellite to a planet to learn more. The satellite travels across space to the planet. Then it goes into orbit around the planet and sends back to Earth pictures and other information.

*◄ An image from the Hubble telescope*

# When Satellites Fall

Satellites cannot stay in orbit around Earth forever. Satellites get old. What happens then?

An old satellite starts to slow down. Then it begins to fall to Earth. It falls faster and faster as it gets closer to the ground. It starts to burn up as it streaks through the air. Sometimes it burns up completely. Other times, a part of it falls into the ocean. A new satellite is usually ready to go up and take its place.

◀ *A new satellite is sent into space.*

## Glossary

**altitude**—the height of something above the ground

**galaxies**—large groups of stars

**global positioning system (GPS)**—a system of satellites used to tell positioning on Earth

**orbit**—to travel around a planet

**solar panels**—a system that turns sunlight into electricity to power equipment

## Did You Know?

- Earth is a satellite of the sun and the moon is a satellite of Earth.
- A satellite must reach an **altitude** of at least 120 miles (193 kilometers) and a speed of more than 18,000 miles (28,962 kilometers) per hour to lift into orbit.
- Some satellites are launched in space by astronauts aboard a space shuttle. A space shuttle can also bring satellites back to Earth if they need to be repaired.

# Want to Know More?

## At the Library

Ganeri, Anita. *The Story of Communications*. New York: Oxford University Press
   Children's Books, 1998.
Walker, Niki and Kalman, Bobbie. *Satellites and Space Probes*. New York: Crabtree Publishing, 1998.

## On the Web

**The Satellite Site**
*http://www.thetech.org/exhibits_events/online/satellite/*
For information about satellites and a program that lets you put together your own satellite

**Beginner's Guide to Observing Satellites**
*http://www2.satellite.eu.org/sat/vsohp/beginner.html*
For a beginner's guide to observing satellites in the night sky. Ask an adult to help you look
for satellites with information from this site.

**NASA Satellite Images**
*http://observe.ivv.nasa.gov/nasa/gallery/world/world_1.html*
For pictures of the Earth taken by the Landsat satellites

## Through the Mail

**National Aeronautics and Space Administration (NASA)**
Headquarters Information Center
Washington, DC 20546-0001
For more information about NASA's space research

## On the Road

**National Air and Space Museum**
Located on the National Mall
7th Street and Independence Avenue, S.W.
Washington, DC 20560-0321
To tour the museum and learn more about the history of air and space travel

23

# Index

## About the Author

Darlene R. Stille is a science editor and writer. She has lived in Chicago, Illinois, all her life. When she was in high school, she fell in love with science. While attending the University of Illinois, she discovered that she also enjoyed writing. Today she feels fortunate to have a career that allows her to pursue both her interests. Darlene R. Stille has written more than thirty books for young people.